Captain Thunderbolt

Australian Bushrangers
Jane Smith

EasyRead Large

Copyright Page from the Original Book

Big Sky Publishing Pty Ltd
PO Box 303, Newport, NSW 2106, Australia
Phone: 1300 364 611
Fax: (61 2) 9918 2396
Email: info@bigskypublishing.com.au
Web: www.bigskypublishing.com.au

Cover design and typesetting: Think Productions

National Library of Australia Cataloguing-in-Publication entry
Author: Smith, Jane Margaret.
Title: Captain Thunderbolt / Jane Smith.
ISBN: 9781922132574 (paperback)
Series: Australian bushrangers.
Target Audience: For primary school age.
Subjects: Thunderbolt, 1835-1870--Juvenile literature.
          Bushrangers--New South Wales--History--Juvenile literature.
Dewey Number: 364.1552092

TABLE OF CONTENTS

I would like to thank historian Carol Baxter (author of Captain Thunderbolt and his lady) for her generous advice, fact-checking and proof-reading. I would also like to thank Ken Mayo of McCrossin's Mill Museum and Arnold Goode of the Uralla Historical Society for their assistance and support on this project.

1

THE BEGINNING

The legend

In the New South Wales country town of Uralla stands a life-sized statue of the bushranger "Captain Thunderbolt" mounted upon a horse. Thunderbolt was a horse thief, a highwayman – a criminal. Why is he honoured in this way? The answer lies in all the stories that have surrounded his life – stories of a loving husband and father, a gentleman, a lover of music and literature; a man who hated violence and was treated unfairly by the law. There are so many stories that it is difficult to separate fact from fiction. Thunderbolt himself was a storyteller, fond of bragging about his adventures to his victims. The truth, however, is quite a different story.

Early life

"Captain Thunderbolt" was the alias of Frederick Wordsworth Ward. Born in 1835, Fred was the youngest son of English ex-convict Michael (also known as Handley Thompson) and Sophia Ward. Michael had been convicted of theft and transported to Australia; his wife followed him as a free woman, with their daughter Sophia. It was not long before Michael gained his ticket-of-leave and the family settled in the village of Wilberforce, west of Sydney. About the time their eleventh child, Fred, was born, the family moved a few miles away to Windsor. By then, Fred's second eldest sister Sarah was a grown woman with two sons – James and John Garbutt – who would play an important part in Fred's life.

Statue of Thunderbolt on his horse at Uralla, NSW. Photo courtesy of author.

We know very little about Fred's early life. It is likely that he had little schooling; when he was arrested at the age of twenty Fred was able to read a little but not to write.

By the age of ten or eleven he was living in the Maitland region and already working as a station hand.

Fred was very good with horses. When he was only a young man he was known as one of the best horse-breakers in the district. He travelled widely around the colony, working in stations all around New South Wales. He came to know the land thoroughly; this was a knowledge that served him well in his later years as a bushranger.

Currency lads

"Currency lads" – children of ex-convicts like Fred Ward – were often despised by the wealthy free settlers. In turn they became resentful of authority; they were proud of their bush skills and knowledge of the land and scorned the refinements of British-born immigrants. They valued courage and physical strength over education.

Fred's parents lived out the rest of their lives in Maitland. His father died in 1859 but his mother Sophia lived until 1874, by which time her infamous son was dead.

2

THE APPRENTICE

The first crime

In March 1856, when Fred was about 20, he mustered cattle for two weeks on Tocal Station in the Hunter Valley for a man named Charles Reynolds. Fred and his brother William had both worked as stockmen and horse-breakers on the station before, as had their older brother George.

Fred's nephew John Garbutt already had a big "business" in horse and cattle theft, and was wanted by police for stealing horses in Queensland. In April 1856 Fred joined John and his brother James Garbutt to take part in a crime that would change the course of his life. The Garbutts stole a mob of horses from Fred's former employer at Tocal and from a neighbouring station and took them to a property leased by William Ward and his business partner Michael Blake. From there Fred, John Garbutt and an Aboriginal servant drove the horses to auction in Windsor.

The horses were sold, but unfortunately for the thieves, someone recognised the horses as being stolen property. The men were promptly arrested.

Why Fred became involved in this crime has long been a mystery. Did he take on the mustering job with the intention of robbing his employer? Some say that the Ward family attacked Tocal Station in revenge for the death of Fred's brother George. George had drowned in floodwaters in 1854 when taking a herd of Mr Reynolds' cattle to Maitland. However, if the Wards blamed Reynolds for George's death, it would not explain why they stole most of the horses from his neighbour William Zuill. It is more likely that Fred, like his nephews, was simply attracted to the idea of easy money.

Indeed, only a few months earlier he had been arrested for droving stolen cattle; although he was acquitted of the crime, his presence suggests that Fred's behaviour may not have been completely lawful. At the very least, he was beginning to keep dishonest company. One thing is certain: this crime would be the first step in the transformation of Fred Ward, horse breaker, into Thunderbolt, the bushranger.

A cottage at Tocal homestead, NSW. Fred Ward worked at Tocal in 1856. He is believed to have lived

in this cottage. Photo from the website: www.tocal. com

Sentenced, imprisoned and freed

John and James Garbutt were convicted of horse-stealing and sentenced to 10 years' imprisonment with hard labour on Cockatoo Island. The court was unable to prove that Fred was involved in the theft. He was instead found guilty of "receiving" the stolen horses and given the same harsh sentence as his nephews.

On 27 August 1856 Ward arrived on Cockatoo Island. He served four years of his sentence before being released on a "ticket-of-leave" on 1 July 1860. James Garbutt was freed at about the same time and John a month later. John soon married a wealthy widow and the pair settled on her station at Cooyal, near Mudgee. Soon afterwards, Fred began work as a stockman for the new Mrs Garbutt. It was there that he fell in love with Mary Ann Bugg. Mary Ann was a well-educated part-Aboriginal woman who was to become Thunderbolt's partner in crime and in love for many years to come.

Fred's freedom, however, was short-lived.

Ten Pounds Reward.

THE following HORSE STOCK, supposed to have been STOLEN from Belle Vue, on the 21st of last month, are still amissing—

One chestnut mare, branded WZ, and numbered, with chesnut foal at foot

One bay mare, WZ near shoulder

One bay mare, aged, WZ near shoulder, TL off neck

One bay colt, star, Z near shoulder

One grey yearling filly, Z near shoulder

One large bay mare, very heavy boned, NK near shoulder, with other brands, had a large bay filly foal at foot unbranded

One bay filly, star, both hind feet white, branded small JN near shoulder

One black filly, near hind foot white, small JN near shoulder

One bay yearling pony filly, HL under saddle near side

One bay mare, F near shoulder, has a bay horse foal, with white strip down his face, at foot.

A reward of One Pound each will be paid on delivery of either of the above horses to the undersigned, and if found in possession of any one after this notice they will be dealt with as the law directs. Any information that may lead to their recovery will be thankfully received.

3088   WILLIAM ZUILL.

A report of the theft of horses from William Zuill. From the Maitland Mercury & Hunter River General Advertiser 24 May 1856, Trove Newspapers, NLA Article 18655258.

Return to Cockatoo Island

Soon after they met, Mary Ann fell pregnant with Fred's child, and he took her to her father's home near Dungog to prepare for the birth of the baby. By doing so, Fred was breaking the conditions of his ticket-of-leave.

Cockatoo Island in the background, pictured before 1864. State Library of NSW SPF/817.

When prisoners were released on tickets-of-leave, they had to remain in the district to which they were assigned. Another condition was that they "attend muster" – or report to the police – at regular times. When Fred Ward failed to show up to muster in Mudgee on 13 September 1861 his ticket-of-leave was cancelled and Fred was once again a "wanted" man. Worse than that, when he did arrive in Mudgee six days later he was also charged with stealing the horse that he was riding. Although he claimed to have bought the horse he could not prove it and was immediately sentenced to serve out the rest of his term (six years) on Cockatoo Island. On top of that, another three years were added for horse theft.

On 26 October 1861, while Fred waited in Mudgee Gaol, Mary Ann gave birth to their first child, Marina Emily Ward. By early November Fred Ward was back on Cockatoo Island.

Escape

Cockatoo Island

Located in Sydney Harbour, Cockatoo Island was one of Australia's harshest prisons. The prisoners were put to work on sandstone quarries, some shackled in leg irons. Their thin clothing did little to keep out the cold and they were fed meagre rations of bread and meat. Prisoners were locked up for 12 hours at night in poorly ventilated, overcrowded and stinking dormitories. The solitary confinement cells were tiny, dark pits cut into the sandstone, capped by heavy stone "lids".

During his first imprisonment on Cockatoo Island, Fred had kept out of trouble. On only one occasion was he put into a solitary confinement cell for three days. When he returned in 1861, however, he was involved in acts of rebellion against changes in the prison system. For refusing to work, for disobedience and for causing disturbances he was sentenced several times to solitary confinement, although due to a lack of available cells he was spared that punishment.

Cockatoo Island was a cruel prison full of desperate men. Riots and attempts at escape were frequent but always failed. Then on 11 September 1863, Fred Ward and another convict, Fred Britten, became the first and only prisoners ever to escape successfully from Cockatoo Island.

The island was heavily guarded by land and by sea, and surrounded by sharks. In spite of this, Fred Ward and Fred Britten managed to escape.

£50 REWARD.—Whereas, on the 11th September last, two convicts, named FREDERICK BRITTAIN and FREDERICK WARD, effected their escape from the penal establishment at Cockatoo Island: Notice is hereby given that a reward of twenty-five pounds will be paid by the Government to any person who may first give such information as shall lead to the re-apprehension of each of the offenders.

CHARLES COWPER.

Colonial Secretary's Office, Sydney, 12th October, 1863.

DESCRIPTION OF ESCAPED PRISONERS.

Brittain is a native of Hobart Town; a labourer, 28 years of age, 5 feet 8 inches high, fair ruddy complexion, light brown hair, and hazel eyes.

Ward is a native of Windsor, New South Wales; a labourer, twenty-seven years of age, 5 foot 8½ inches high, pale sallow complexion, light brown curly hair, hazel grey eyes, mole on right wrist, and two warts back of middle finger of left hand.   1391.

Reward for the capture of the escapees, from Bell's Life in Sydney and Sporting Chronical 17 Oct 1863. Accessed from Trove newspapers 59793915/3.

Myth: the escape

There are plenty of stories about the escape, though none have been proven. Years later Mary Ann claimed that she got work as a housemaid in Balmain, near Cockatoo Island, and that she swam out to the island with food for Ward and a file to cut the chains of his partner. Then as the men swam to the mainland under cover of night, she guided them with a lamp to shore. This story cannot be true as Mary Ann was working far away in Dungog at the time. The men probably hid somewhere on the island for a couple of days before swimming north to Woolwich under cover of darkness.

When the guards realised the men were missing, they searched the island. They found Britten's leg irons and some of the prisoners' clothes, but no trace of the men. A reward of £25 was offered for their capture.

Ward and Britten travelled north together. The two men robbed a hut on Gostwyck Station near Uralla, stealing a gun and some meat. A few days later they set out to hold up the mail at "Big Rock", just south of Uralla. Knowing that the robbers were in the area, however, two troopers travelled with the mailman to guard him. They came upon the bushrangers and fired. The two men fled; Fred Ward was shot in the left knee but managed to escape through the scrub. After a couple of weeks the escapees separated, with Fred making his way to the Hunter Valley and Britten possibly heading to Victoria. "Big Rock", where Thunderbolt was shot, later became known as "Thunderbolt's Rock".

Fred Britten

Fred Ward befriended Fred Britten while they were both imprisoned on Cockatoo Island. Britten had been arrested in late 1862 for robbery, and sentenced to 16 years with hard labour, with the first year in leg irons.

He had made three previous attempts at escape. The first was immediately after his arrest, when he made a run for it as he was being taken to the Police Office. The second was when he took off outside Darlinghurst Gaol, and the third was an attempt to break out of his ward on Cockatoo Island.

"Big Rock", also known as "Split Rock" near Uralla, where Thunderbolt's bushranging career began and ended. It is now known as "Thunderbolt's Rock". Photo courtesy of author.

The bushranging epidemic

Social conditions of the mid-nineteenth century were largely to blame for the "epidemic" of bushranging. Poor small farmers struggled to make ends meet and many survived by stealing stock from their richer neighbours. With properties unfenced and no register of stock brands, this was easy to do. In rural areas, too, police were few and communications poor; life was tough and crime was common.

Children in the bush often grew up without education and therefore without the means to improve their lives. The children of ex-convicts were resentful of their wealthier neighbours and distrustful of the law. Many struggling farmers could sympathise with men who ranged the bush stealing horses or cattle; they saw themselves as being on the same side in the fight against the authorities.

Mary Ann Bugg

As the daughter of an Aboriginal woman, Mary Ann Bugg had skills that made her an ideal companion for a bushranger. She knew the land and she could track, hunt and survive in the bush.

Born on 7 May 1834, Mary Ann was the first child of James and Charlotte Bugg. James was an ex-convict who had been transported for life for stealing lambs, a sheep and two pigs. He was assigned to work as a shepherd for the Australian Agricultural Company. In time he was promoted to overseer in the isolated Gloucester region, and received his "ticket-of-leave" in 1834. James and Charlotte Bugg had eight children together; they married in 1848 after their seventh child was born.

Photo courtesy of Kent Mayo, McCrossin's Mill Museum.

Mary Ann was unusually well-educated for a woman of her race and class at the time. Her father had sent Mary Ann and her brother John to school in Sydney where she learned to read, write, cook and sew. Her parents wanted to bring their children up in a way that would allow them to leave behind the "savage life". Mary Ann stayed at the school for five years before returning to her family at the age of ten.

In 1848 Mary Ann married Edmund Baker, a forty-year-old shepherd and former convict. She was only fourteen years old. With Edmund she seems to have had one child – a daughter. By 1851, however, Mary Ann was living with another shepherd named John Burrows. What became of Edmund Baker – whether he died or separated from her – is unknown. Mary Ann had two children with Burrows before separating from him and moving on to a relationship with James McNally. Mary Ann and James had a further three children. Fred Ward would be her fourth "husband".

Mary Ann is said to have been a beautiful and graceful woman. According to police records, she was five feet two and a half inches tall, with dark-sallow complexion, black hair, brown eyes and a nose "slightly cocked". She referred proudly to herself as "Mrs Thunderbolt, the captain's lady." Mary Ann's education and her Aboriginal heritage had prepared her well for both European and Indigenous societies, and yet as a "half-caste" she would be fully accepted by neither. It was perhaps for this reason that she surrendered her "respectable" life to live the dangerous and harsh life of a bushranger's mate.

3

THE FULL-TIME BUSHRANGER

The first hold-up

Before dawn on 21 December 1863, William Delaney was at work in the toll-house at Campbell's Hill, near Rutherford, when a man slipped into the room and pointed a revolver at him. The stranger demanded money. Delaney replied that he had none.

Legend: the name

A story is often told that Captain Thunderbolt got his name during this encounter. The story goes that the first warning Delaney got of the intruder was a pounding on the door. The noise, Delaney exclaimed, was like thunder. To which the bushranger supposedly replied:

"And so it is. I am the thunder, and this (his pistol) is my bolt!" This is one of the many myths that grew up around Thunderbolt; like many others, it is a good story but probably untrue.

A sketch of Thunderbolt from The Truth, 21 February 1892.

Captain Thunderbolt, as he would soon become known, searched the room until he found a cashbox with a few shillings in it; he took the cashbox, wished Delaney a "good morning" and rode away.

Thunderbolt made his way to the Spread Eagle Inn at Rutherford, where he ordered bread and meat and chatted with the customers. When he asked the landlady, Mrs Byrne, how much he should pay, she replied that there was no charge. He responded: "I came to rob you, but as you are so hospitable I won't do so." He bought some rum and left.

Sometime later Delaney made his way to the Spread Eagle Inn. On his way he came upon the bushranger, who remarked "Well, you are the chap I stuck up this morning at the toll-bar. I suppose you have come after me!" Delaney replied that he had not; he was on his way to the inn. Thunderbolt then returned the money he had taken from Delaney, saying: "I am a bushranger, and you might meet a worse one than me; I was put on a lay to stick up your place, I was told there were 200 sovereigns there. I thought it was Young, the flash fighting man, who kept the place; if I met him, I'd take it out of him." He then told Delaney where to find the cashbox and continued on his way.

On the road a little while later, Thunderbolt bailed up a Mr Godfrey Parsons and his wife. He demanded money, but Parsons (though he had much more) claimed to have only £2. He was taking his wife to the doctor in Maitland, he said, and begged the bushranger to leave her alone. Thunderbolt let them go without taking their money, declaring that he would not rob a sick woman.

He spent the rest of the day on the road, sometimes stopping to have tea or a chat with travellers, robbing some and letting others go. At one point, Constable Edward Purcell arrived on foot to investigate reports of the toll-bar robbery. Ward challenged the policeman, asking: "Don't you want me?", but Purcell did not arrest him. The policeman was later charged with neglect of duty, fined and dismissed.

Thunderbolt rode back to the Spread Eagle Inn, where he had some tea, bread and milk, and bragged about his exploits to the customers. After he had left the Inn, four troopers arrived to look for him, and soon were on their way in pursuit of the bushranger. They found him chatting to a farmer by the road. The constable pointed his revolver at Ward and said "You are my prisoner!" Thunderbolt, however, replied "Am I?", and galloped away. The troopers followed and fired at him but after a long chase, Thunderbolt disappeared into the bush.

Police description

The NSW Police Gazette of 14/10/1863 describes Fred Ward as follows:

Ward is a native of Windsor, New South Wales; a laborer, 27 years of age, five feet 8 ¼ inches high, pale sallow complexion, light brown curly hair, hazel grey eyes, mole on right wrist and two warts back of middle finger of left hand.

On the run

Although Thunderbolt was to have the longest "career" of any of the Australian bushrangers, it got off to a slow start. His first day of highway robbery was not very successful, and afterward little was heard of Thunderbolt for over a year. By early 1864 he had returned to Dungog to fetch Mary Ann and take her with him up to the Culgoa River, northwest of Walgett. It was a three-month journey through the mountainous region now known as Barrington Tops and then inland up towards the Queensland border. They brought with them their daughter Marina and another daughter: Ellen, Mary Ann's youngest child by James McNally. They remained in the Culgoa for eight months, keeping to themselves and hidden from police.

The newspapers reported a number of sightings – though how many were "real" it is impossible to say. Some reported having seen Thunderbolt carrying his children in wickerwork baskets attached to his horse. By this time it was impossible for Ward to slip back into society and enjoy an "honest" family life. He was reported to have said "They would not leave me alone when I was quiet, so I was determined to go out and torment them."

4

THE GANG

Accomplices

By early 1865 Thunderbolt had come out of his "retirement" and joined forces with three other men: "McIntosh", John Thompson, and a man known as "The Bull".

Partners in crime

Thomas Hogan, otherwise known as **"The Bull"** or **"The Bully"** or **Thomas Healey,** was a labourer born in Maitland. He was the first to join Thunderbolt's "gang".

McIntosh was a tall and very thin Scottish man with a sandy complexion and fair hair. He was said to be fond of dancing.

John Thompson was only about 17 years old when he stole a horse, threatened to shoot his employer, and rode off to become a bushranger. He had been employed on a station near Moree and was very skilled with horses. One observer described him as "fair hair, no beard, about five feet 8 or 9 inches high, very stupid looking".

Together the men travelled widely, north to the Queensland border, south to the Tamworth district and almost as far west as Bourke. They robbed travellers, stations and stores; they stole money, weapons, food and clothing. They also took horses and saddles. Thunderbolt had a special liking for fine racehorses.

John Thompson, one of Thunderbolt's earlier accomplices. Photo Carol Baxter's website. Details at www.thunderboltbushranger.com.au.

In March 1865 the police came close to capturing Thunderbolt. With the help of a black tracker, Sergeant Cleary of the Bourke police discovered Thunderbolt's family at the bushranger's camp site at Narran Lake, about 100 miles from Bourke. Since Thunderbolt himself was nowhere to be seen, Cleary instead arrested Mary Ann for having stolen goods in her possession. Mary Ann "sprang like a tigress upon one of the police, ribboning his uniform, and taunting him with cowardice for seeking her apprehension instead of Thunderbolt's". Mary Ann was heavily pregnant and, believing that she was in labour, Cleary took her and the children into custody at Wilby Wilby Station on the Narran River before leaving to search for Thunderbolt. Two days later, however, Thunderbolt and his gang showed up at the station to free her. They fetched Mary Ann and the children and demanded gunpowder. Gunpowder, they told their victims, was "of more value to them than gold". Later the gang returned to the station to eat supper and help themselves to cash and other supplies.

IX.

Miscellaneous Information.

Information has been received that a man known as Dav .. Thunderbolt, but who is believed to be identical with Frederick Ward, escaped prisoner from the Penal Establishment, Cockatoo Island (*Vide Police Gazette*, 16th September, 1863, page 279, p. VI), has been living for the last six months on the Culgoa, with a half-caste girl and two children; he left there about 5 weeks ago, supposed for the purpose of stealing horses from Mr. Reynolds' station on the Paterson, and which he will no doubt take to Queensland. It is more than probable that he will return to the Culgoa, to rejoin the half-caste. He left behind a favorite racing mare.

A report on Thunderbolt's movements from NSW Police Gazette 25 Jan 1965. p.32.

Myth: an unarmed bushranger

One of the myths about Thunderbolt is that he disliked guns and never fired at anyone. However, many of his victims reported that Thunderbolt was heavily armed. It is true that he never killed anyone, but more than once the bushranger fired at police and missed his target. The truth is that Fred Ward was a clever man. He realised that he had a better chance of survival if he simply escaped on his racehorse than if he stayed to fight. The police had poor quality horses and guns and what is more, they had little or no training in how to use their weapons. It is unlikely that a man who hated guns would value gunpowder more highly than gold!

Sergeant Cleary in 1912. Cleary was the policeman who came close to capturing Thunderbolt in 1865. When Thunderbolt escaped, Clearly arrested Mary Ann instead. Trove newspapers, Story of a Pioneer, Career of Ex-senior Sergeant Cleary 12411107.

Having freed Mary Ann from the clutches of the police, Thunderbolt took her south back to the Tamworth district. It was there, in mid-1865, that Mary Ann gave birth to another child. She named their daughter Eliza.

The captive woman

Thunderbolt hired a part Aboriginal woman to look after Mary Ann during her pregnancy. Much later – in March 1866 – this woman turned up in Stroud and claimed that after the child was born, Thunderbolt had forced her to stay with them. She stated that the bushranger had kept her tied to a tree to prevent escape. Her claims that Thunderbolt had kept her captive were never proven.

The Warialda Mail

With Mary Ann settled near Tamworth after the birth of their child, Thunderbolt and his gang travelled widely and embarked on a wild and reckless crime spree.

On the morning of 19 April 1865, not far from Manilla, Thunderbolt, McIntosh and Thompson bailed up the Warialda Mail and threatened Martin Hurley (the driver) with their revolvers. Then while McIntosh guarded the mailman, the other two rode back along the road to hold up a buggy driven by Mr Ross. Thunderbolt said politely to him: "I must trouble you, Sir, to bail up". He asked Mr Ross for money but Ross replied that he had none, and begged Thunderbolt not to frighten his passenger Mrs Redhead. Thunderbolt assured Mr Ross that he "never molested a lady, nor would he allow any one with him to do so".

The "Gentleman"

Thunderbolt had a reputation for being polite to his victims. He was especially gallant to women and prided himself on never robbing a woman.

Thunderbolt and his companion returned to Mr Hurley and rifled through the mail. They took all the cash, cheques and gold that they could find, but returned letters to the mailman. This was to become a pattern for Thunderbolt; he was not interested in the letters – only the money.

At the time when bushrangers were such a menace on the roads, if people had to mail cash or cheques they would often cut them in half and mail each half separately. This would make them useless to bushrangers and thus discourage robbery. Thunderbolt, however, would steal even the half-notes, claiming that he would get the other halves next time.

The robbers took Mr Hurley's waistcoat and gold watch, but later returned them to him. Before leaving they took the mailman's horse for their "mate" ("The Bull") who was waiting in the bush.

The reader

When he held up mail coaches, as well as stealing money, Thunderbolt would sometimes also take newspapers. He liked to read reports of his crimes in them. Once he complained to a victim that there was not much to read out in the bush.

Capture of Thompson

Over the next few days the gang made their way to Mr Cheeseborough's Station "Tareela" near Barraba, stealing race horses from properties along their way. From Tareela they stole a horse, a revolver and some food. One of the women scolded Thunderbolt for his behaviour and he left without searching the house.

The police were once more on Thunderbolt's trail. Martin Hurley had advised the Tamworth police of the mail robbery and Constables Dalton and Lynch set out in pursuit. Over the next few days more crimes were committed. The gang held up Munro's Inn at Boggy Creek, where they drank heavily and took about £50 in cash and more in goods. Mr Munro challenged them to a fight, but the drunken intruders laughed at him and shot his dog. They moved on then to Mr Walford's Inn at Millie. Mr Walford, however, had been warned of their approach and hidden his valuables.

By this time Constable Norris of Barraba and a black tracker had joined the hunt, and the police had followed the gang to Walford's Inn. The bushrangers saw them coming and mounted their horses; Thunderbolt rode out to the field, waving his revolver as if inviting the police to follow him. Once all were out in the open, Thunderbolt fired and then began a shoot-out that lasted for about an hour. A police bullet hit Thompson in the back and came out his stomach; Thompson fell but raised his gun to aim at Dalton. Before he could fire, Norris shot Thompson through the neck and jaw.

Thunderbolt made a few attempts to rescue the boy but had to retreat from police gunfire. He and the others escaped into the bush while the police turned their attention to Thompson.

Surprisingly, the boy survived. He was tried and sentenced to fifteen years' imprisonment with hard labour.

The police had failed to capture Thunderbolt but they had made one arrest and succeeded in breaking up the gang. Sometime after this incident, McIntosh and "The Bull" parted from their leader. Thunderbolt returned to Mary Ann and the children to move them to a camp near the Borah Ranges. They needed to always keep one step ahead of the police.

John Thompson

John Thompson was released in 1872, but only months later was arrested again for burglary and sentenced to ten years imprisonment. He was released in 1881 but the following year was imprisoned once again for trying to rob a bank.

Thomas Hogan

"The Bull" (Thomas Hogan) was captured in 1866 after bailing up a publican in Queensland. He served three months' imprisonment in Rockhampton, and then was sent back to NSW to face trial for the crimes committed with Thunderbolt. He was sentenced to 17 years but served only 11.

5

THE SECOND GANG

The crimes continue

Although he now was caring for three children, Thunderbolt was not about to take a break. On 9 August 1865 he held up the Warialda-Tamworth mail at Oakey Creek. It was driven by Martin Hurley, the same mailman whom Thunderbolt had robbed near Manilla only a few months earlier. Again Hurley informed the police, and again Constable Dalton set out to look for him – but again failed to capture the bushranger.

By October Thunderbolt had found some new accomplices, and together over the next few months they robbed hotels, a mail coach, stores and stations, travelling over the border into Queensland. His "partners in crime" were "Jemmy the Whisperer" and Patrick Kelly.

Patrick Kelly

Patrick John Kelly was born in Ireland and migrated to Australia as a child with his family. The Maitland Mercury described him as "a fine-made man, in height about six feet, black full beard, about thirty-seven years of age, and very respectable in appearance."

Jemmy the Whisperer

In 1866 The Maitland Mercury described Jemmy, or James Bell, as "about 5 feet 4, grey eyes, with light hair rather inclined to curl, had a slight limp in his walk; wore cord breeches, long boots, light colour thick coat, new Cabbage-tree hat with velvet round it; age about 30." When he joined Thunderbolt he was wanted by police for the shooting of Constable Rayfield.

Jemmy was said to be a fine singer. Jemmy and Kelly once held up the publican of the Pine Ridge hotel, stealing £7, and then staying for hours to boast of their adventures, sing, and drink. The publican reported that the pair sang very well, and that Jemmy, in particular, sang so well that he had "never heard better, or I may even say his equal, in any theatre."

Crime wave of December 1865

The end of 1865 was a busy time for Thunderbolt and his partners.

On 8 December 1865 Thunderbolt and his new gang committed perhaps the most daring of their crimes.

At around 11am the trio rode into the small town of Quirindi on stolen racehorses and made their way to Benjamin Cook's Inn. They stole four bridles and a saddle, £9 in cash, some clothing, soap and perfume from the store, and two horses from customer Mr Ross. Then they joined the customers to drink and chat and brag about their crimes. When Mr Davis arrived, the bushrangers ordered him to hand over his saddle but he refused and put up a struggle. Thunderbolt threatened to shoot him but did not follow through with his threat. He let Davis go and the bushrangers stayed till the afternoon, buying drinks for the customers and enjoying the company.

Mr Ross's son managed to escape and report the robbery to the police, who set off immediately for the inn. The bushrangers saw the police arriving, however, and wasted no time in mounting their horses and riding away. The police tried to pursue the gang, but their horses were no match for the robbers' racehorses, and when night fell they gave up.

Meanwhile, the bushrangers made their way back to Cook's Inn to continue the fun. Many of the guests stayed on willingly with Thunderbolt and his men, partying until late in the night. At about 11pm, when the police finally returned, the bushrangers bought some more bottles of spirits and quietly slipped away.

The next morning, the gang made their way to Currububula, robbing William Matthews on their way. From Matthews they took a cheque for £16 and a horse, saddle and bridle. The next day Matthews found his horse and saddle in the bush; apparently the horse was not good enough for Thunderbolt.

When they reached Currububula the men bailed up Mr Davis' Inn and all who were in it. They put the guests into the front parlour while they searched the place and found about £18 in cash and cheques, and a saddle of Mr Davis's. They then ordered breakfast, which they ate with the family; they drank some ale, and left with some tea and sugar from the store.

The following day the gang headed to Carroll, where they robbed the mailman before turning up at Griffin's Inn. A thunderstorm was under way and many travellers were waiting out the storm at the inn. Kelly arrived first, dismounting and entering the bar for a drink. A little while later the guests watched as another two men arrived on horseback, each leading a spare horse. As they entered the verandah they drew out their pistols and said politely "I will trouble you all, ladies and gentlemen, to bail up". They reassured the frightened women that no one would be hurt; they only wanted money. The bushrangers lined up all the guests and staff and searched the pockets of the men. They took cash from some of the captives, as well as a watch and chain from one man, which they later returned.

Their "work" done, the robbers ordered Mr De Vere to play the violin, while Kelly danced with one of the ladies. The bushrangers bought drinks all round and encouraged the customers to enjoy themselves.

The storyteller

Thunderbolt was a great storyteller. He was known to hold up an inn and while holding the customers captive, would entertain them for hours with stories of his exploits.

The party lasted until around 9pm when Senior Constable Lang, Constable Aggett and Constable Shaw arrived. They were seeking a bed for the night and had no idea that a holdup was in progress, until the landlord quietly let them know what was happening. Thunderbolt, realising that police were present, mounted his horse and tried to flee. Constable Lang fired, and Jemmy, who was still on foot, returned his fire, wounding Lang in the right arm. The injury was not serious but it gave the bushrangers a chance to escape, and once more they disappeared into the bush.

Thunderbolt and his gang finished off 1865 with a spate of crimes in and around Collarenebri. They robbed several stations, a pub, an inn and a store. The reward for Thunderbolt's capture was increased to £100.

> CAPTAIN THUNDERBOLT —We observe that a reward of £100 is offered by the Government for the apprehension of Frederick Ward (otherwise known as " Thunderbolt"), and a reward of £30 for the apprehension of any of his accomplices. If the apprehension should be effected upon information received, one-half of the reward in either case will be given to the person giving the information, and the other half to the person or persons effecting the capture.

The reward for Thunderbolt's capture increased to £100. Notice in The Maitland Mercury & Hunter River General Advertiser 7 Dec 1865. Trove newspapers 187000003/3.

Then in January 1866, for reasons unknown, Thunderbolt and his second gang went their separate ways.

Driven to crime

Thunderbolt sometimes complained to his victims that he no longer had a choice but to continue bushranging. Once, when robbing the Chambers family at the Meroe Inn, the young Miss Chambers asked him, "Why do you want to rob anyone? Why don't you get work and earn an honest living?" Thunderbolt replied: "I can't Miss Chambers, whenever I take a job the police hear of it, and I'm hounded down by the authorities".

The fates of Jemmy and Kelly

After parting from Thunderbolt, Jemmy and Kelly carried on with their robberies for another month.

Their spree came to an end in February 1866, when the police noticed Kelly lurking about an inn at Collarenebri. They traced him to his campsite and fired at him. Kelly almost escaped by swimming across a river, but later that day he was found by a tracker and arrested. He was sentenced to 19 years' imprisonment. In 1873 he was released to be exiled to America.

Jemmy, on the other hand, remained free for many years. It was not until 1882 that a man named James Bell, believed to have been Thunderbolt's accomplice "Jemmy the Whisperer" was captured by Senior-Constable Lynch near Walgett and charged with horse-stealing. He was reported to have been the ringleader of a group of horse thieves who had been operating in the Walgett region for several years. He was also accused of having shot Constable Rayfield back in 1866.

6

NEAR CAPTURE

Mary Ann arrested again … and again

In early 1866, now parted from his gang, Thunderbolt was once more on the move with Mary Ann and the three children. With them came the woman who had been employed to help Mary Ann through childbirth. Then on 22 March the woman turned up at the police station in Stroud. She claimed to have escaped from Thunderbolt nine days earlier and offered to lead them to the bushranger's camp.

With the help of a black tracker, the police eventually found their way to Thunderbolt's campsite in the mountains above Gloucester. They surprised the bushranger near his camp and ordered him to "stand". Thunderbolt, however, ignored the command, climbed onto the horse and fled, leaving Mary Ann behind.

The police took Mary Ann and her three children into custody. Mary Ann escaped but was soon recaptured. The police charged her with Vagrancy – of being "an idle and disorderly person and a companion of reputed thieves, and having no visible means of support, or fixed place of residence".

Mary Ann, the rider

When captured, Mary Ann was wearing men's clothing and rode "as men usually do". That is, she did not ride side-saddle, as was usual for women at the time.

Mary Ann was sentenced to six months imprisonment in Maitland Gaol. Many in the community were angered by the sentence, for the Vagrancy Act did not apply to Aboriginal people living in the bush. Some protested that as an Aborigine she could not be charged with vagrancy; others argued that as an educated "half-caste", her Aboriginality could not be used as a defence, and that as an accomplice of an infamous bushranger, Mary Ann deserved to go to gaol.

THE IMPRISONMENT OF MRS. THUNDER-BOLT.

To the Editor of the Herald.

Sir,—In your issue of to-day I notice an abstract from the Maitland Mercury, of the 31st ultimo, to the effect that Mrs. Thunderbolt has been apprehended and sentenced to six months' imprisonment under the Vagrant Act. My object in writing to you is to express an opinion—which I think must be that of the public as well—that this unfortunate woman suffers in being so imprisoned for the deeds of her reputed husband; and committals of this kind only bring law into contempt.

I am, Sir, yours, &c.
A LOVER OF JUSTICE.

This letter to the editor in the Sydney Morning Herald of 7 April 1966 shows the public objections to the imprisonment of Mary Ann Bugg. NLA Trove 13129118/3.

It was not only the public who were outraged. The matter was argued in Parliament, until eventually the pressure was enough to make the NSW Governor review the case. Two weeks after she had been imprisoned, Mary Ann was freed from gaol.

Wolfe and Gorrick's store, Maitland, from which Mary Ann Bugg bought the fabric she was accused of stealing. Courtesy of Cultural Collections (Auchmuty Library), University of Newcastle (Australia).

After her release Mary Ann stayed with Thunderbolt's family and had no contact with him for several months. For most of that year Thunderbolt committed few crimes. Sometime in the middle of that year Mary Ann left her older children with her family and set out to rejoin her lover. It was not long, however, before the police arrested her once again.

On 6 January 1867, a police party came upon Thunderbolt and his family at Allyn Vale, on the Paterson River. Thunderbolt fled as usual on his racehorse, but once again the police captured Mary Ann instead. They searched her saddle bags and found fabric they believed was stolen: calico, Derry cloth and tweed. Mary Ann insisted that she had bought the fabric from Wolfe and Gorrick's store in Maitland, but had no receipts to prove it. She was found guilty of possessing stolen goods and sentenced to three months' imprisonment at Maitland Gaol. When Mary Ann wrote to the NSW Governor protesting her innocence, however, the matter was investigated. It was resolved when the local magistrate questioned the salesman at Wolfe and Gorrick's store. The salesman remembered selling Mary Ann the fabric and proved her innocence. Mary Ann was released on 1 March 1867 and soon rejoined her lover.

Mary Ann, the hunter

Mary Ann helped Thunderbolt steal cattle for their food. She would bind a blade to a long stick and use it cut the leg muscles of the beast as she rode up beside it. Once the animal had fallen she could kill it.

The crimes continue

When Mary Ann was in gaol, her lover became reckless. Sunday, 3 February 1867 was a day of wild and drunken crime for Thunderbolt.

Mailman Abraham Bowden was travelling on horseback to Tamworth, leading a packhorse loaded with the Tamworth-Warialda mail. Mr Dorrington was riding along beside him. They were not far past Manilla when Thunderbolt bailed them up. As usual he was riding a fine racehorse and leading a packhorse.

Thunderbolt ransacked the mail, taking cash and cheques but leaving the letters scattered about on the ground. From the two men he stole money; he also took the mailman's saddle with a promise to return it later. When Thunderbolt had gone, Mr Bowden made his way back to Manilla to borrow a saddle and then continue on his journey to Tamworth. On his way he came upon Senior-Constable Norris and later Constable Shaw and told them about the robbery. They set out in pursuit.

In the meantime Thunderbolt had also ridden into Manilla and was busy holding up an inn. He had bought and drunk large amounts of liquor at Hill's Inn before moving across the road to an inn owned by Mr Veness. When the superintendent of the Manilla pastoral station, Mr McKinnon, arrived on horseback, Thunderbolt pointed a gun to his head. He ordered McKinnon to dismount or he would "blow his brains out". Later Thunderbolt let Mr McKinnon go so that he might continue on his journey to a doctor in Tamworth.

But before McKinnon could leave, Constable Norris arrived on the scene. As usual Thunderbolt mounted his horse quickly and retreated.

Norris followed him; Thunderbolt seemed to vanish but soon reappeared on the other side of the river, laughing drunkenly and taunting the policeman. At that moment Constable Shaw arrived in a buggy to assist, and he and Norris drove together across the river. Thunderbolt tried to bail them up, but when he realised the men were police, he fled and left the packhorse behind. Shaw fired at the bushranger but missed.

Eventually Shaw unhitched his horse from the buggy so that he could chase the bushranger on horseback, but his mount was no match for Thunderbolt's racehorse. Norris had returned to the inn for his horse, only to find that Thunderbolt had taken it by mistake and left his own packhorse behind, loaded with about £427 in stolen cheques.

Sergeant Doherty turned up to help. The three policemen chased and fired upon the bushranger but once again were unable to catch him. Later the newspapers ridiculed the police for their failure and Doherty had Norris charged with neglect of his duty.

7

ANOTHER ACCOMPLICE

Thomas Mason

Shortly before Mary Ann's release, Thunderbolt took on a young accomplice. The young man who would be Thunderbolt's deputy for the next seven months was only fifteen when he was recruited. His name was Thomas Mason.

Thomas Mason

Mason was a boy of about 15 when he teamed up with Thunderbolt. He had already had a hard life: his father was dead and his stepfather was cruel to him. At the age of about 10 he left the orphan school to work as an errand-boy, but later moved to the country to take on a number of short-term jobs. He was on the gold diggings when Fred Ward reportedly rode up, said that he was a squatter and offered Mason a job. Mason eagerly accepted. Later he would claim that he had no idea at first that Ward was a bushranger, but that once he had committed crimes with Ward he was stuck with him.

According to a number of accounts Thomas was not a very bright young man. One newspaper claimed that he was "reported to be half-witted".

Plea for a pardon

On 16 March 1867 Magistrate Lethbridge of Barraba wrote to the Governor Sir John Young with an unusual request: that the Government should offer Fred Ward a pardon. His reasoning was that the bushranger had "never yet shed human blood" and normally showed kindness, politeness and consideration – even to his victims.

There were rumours that Ward was tiring of his lifestyle but unable to change it; Lethbridge warned that if the situation continued, then Ward might yet be driven to violence. He pointed out that Ward's excellent bush skills and horsemanship could be put to better use, and suggested that Ward should be offered a pardon in exchange for a life of service in the police force. Unfortunately for Thunderbolt, the Governor did not agree and no such pardon was offered.

Together Thunderbolt and Mason carried out many robberies of the mail, hotels and stores. Their first exploit was on the Denison goldfields in late February 1867. It nearly resulted in their capture. First they robbed Mr Samuel Cook the store-keeper of £70, and then held up 13 people who were dining in Mr Simpson's Inn. While he bailed up the diners, Thunderbolt sent Mason to search the inn for cash. A man named McInnes arrived at the inn, and seeing that a hold-up was in progress, seized hold of Thunderbolt. A struggle followed; young Mason rushed at McInnes with a knife, and the man let go his grip on the bushranger and fled. Thunderbolt was angry; he ranted against McInnes and swore he would get revenge, saying that "as he was not a blood-thirsty man he would be satisfied with his ears". After a time, however, the robber calmed down, had a few drinks at the bar, and left with Mason, as well as stolen cash and a couple of stolen horses.

A horse drawn mail coach, typical of those used during this period
Powerhouse Museum

Bonshaw Hotel

Another robbery took place in May 1867, when Thunderbolt and Mason held up the hotel in the village of Bonshaw, near the Queensland border. Thunderbolt locked the landlord (James Roper) and his two customers in the hotel's store while he searched the hotel. On finding the safe, Thunderbolt ordered Mr Roper to come out and unlock it for him. The bushranger, Roper said later, was as nervous as the victim: Thunderbolt's hand with the pistol in it trembled. Roper asked him to leave the silver so that he could continue to conduct his business, and so Thunderbolt returned 12 shillings.

He asked for some brandy (and paid for it!), and when he had finished his "work" Thunderbolt sent Mason to free the other victims. They all sat together on the verandah to chat. The bushranger, said Roper, was "prepossessing in appearance, and very agreeable in conversation. He is extremely good in relating narratives of his personal adventures. His feats of horsemanship, narrow escapes of life, were most extraordinary. He has remarkably quick eyes, never for a moment allowing one of us out of sight, and watching all roads at once."

Mr Roper tried to persuade Thunderbolt to give up his dangerous lifestyle "before he got so far as to commit murder"; Thunderbolt thanked him and replied that he had tried it once, but as it didn't work he would not try it again.

The bushrangers, having helped themselves to clothing and a new saddle, money, alcohol, and other items, then said goodbye and left.

Robin Hood

Thunderbolt is sometimes compared – wrongly – with Robin Hood, who stole from the rich to give to the poor. It is true that he often showed pity to his victims and returned his takings. Generally, however, Thunderbolt robbed the rich and poor alike.

Sympathisers

Bushrangers could not survive in the bush or avoid capture without help. Without his supporters, Thunderbolt could never have lasted so long.

Thunderbolt, like most bushrangers, relied on informers to warn him of the movements of the police, and even to lead the police astray in their search for him. Legend has it that people would hang blankets on the washing line to warn Thunderbolt that troopers were nearby. Sympathetic farmers would offer him food, drink and shelter.

Some of these people were paid informers; others were relations or people who felt they had been treated badly by the authorities. Others, fearing for their own safety, would turn a blind eye when the bushranger was in the district.

More robberies with Mason

The next few months were busy for Thunderbolt and Mason; they robbed mail coaches near Manilla, Wallabadah and Murrurrundi. They robbed the Cassilis/Muswellbrook Mail in August and yet again in September. The crime spree continued until September

1867, when Thunderbolt's apprentice Thomas Mason was captured.

An expert horseman

The task of capturing Thunderbolt was almost an impossible one. Thunderbolt rode only the best racehorses while police were equipped with poor horses that were usually already worn out from travelling long distances by the time they found him. The police were criticised for failing to capture the bushranger, but police were few and they struggled to contend with a villain who was an expert horseman and knew the countryside completely.

Mason's capture

In September 1867 Thunderbolt, Mason and Mary Ann were camping in the Borah Ranges. Senior Constables Dalton and Cantrell discovered the bushranger's tracks and followed them through the bush until they came upon his campsite. There they found Thunderbolt himself, sitting down putting his boots on. When he saw the police he ran, leaving one of his boots behind as he sped off into the bush.

Later that day some other policemen came upon Thunderbolt and Mason by chance. They were on horseback, having already stolen more horses to replace the mounts they left behind. The pair escaped again but a few days later they were not so lucky, when the police discovered them with Mary Ann once more. Thunderbolt was still wearing only one shoe. The troopers set off after Thunderbolt, firing as they chased him. Mason rode as hard and as far as he could – about 100 miles – until his horse could carry him no further, and then he continued on foot. The Narribri police, however, soon caught up with him near Millie. Mason was arrested and tried at Tamworth. At his trial, Mason asked the court to consider his youth and troubled childhood. He blamed Fred Ward for leading him unwillingly into a life of crime. He was sentenced to three years' imprisonment.

Attacking the mail (Bushranging, NSW 1864) State Library of Victoria 185989

Thunderbolt Scott
Bill Scott

Thunderbolt came from the Hawkesbury River,

*He was a bushranger, he was a rover;
Made all the rich folk shudder and shiver,
Wore fine clothes and lived in clover.
Riding high on a thoroughbred colt,
Bad man, bushranger, Thunderbolt.*

*Uralla, Armidale, Torrington as well,
Yarrowick Mountain where the farmers dwell,
Saw him pass, till a constable in blue
Caught him and sent him to Cockatoo.
But he broke from his cell and his iron chain
And wandered free in the bush again.*

*He wandered far, he wandered wide,
Nobody knows just where he died
But on Yarrowick Mountain when the moon is high
And misty clouds are drifting by
Riding high on his thoroughbred colt
Comes the ghost of Thunderbolt,
Comes the ghost of Thunderbolt.*

8

DOMESTIC STRIFE

Thunderbolt deserts Mary Ann

There are many stories about the great and lasting love between Thunderbolt and Mary Ann. Sadly, though, the truth is not so romantic. Mary Ann's life with Thunderbolt was terribly hard. She had to raise three children in the bush, always on the run from the law. Twice she was arrested and thrown into prison because of Thunderbolt. Then late in 1867, he left her for another woman.

The woman was Louisa Mason, also known as "Yellow Long." She was the wife of "Cranky" Bob Mason, who was a shepherd at Segenhoe. Like Mary Ann, Louisa was part Aboriginal.

Louisa dies

Thunderbolt's affair with Louisa Mason ended soon after it began – with her death.

In November 1867, a settler named Mrs Bradford was disturbed at her home near Muswellbrook by a knock at her door. The visitor was Thunderbolt. He had called on Mrs Bradford before to purchase supplies, but this time he had a different request. His mistress was dying and he wanted Mrs Bradford to give her shelter and comfort during her final hours. The sick woman was Louisa Mason.

Mrs Bradford agreed to care for her. She followed Thunderbolt's instructions and found where Louisa lay dying of pneumonia in a rough bush camp. Louisa was taken in a cart back to Mrs Bradford's home where, at 9am on Sunday 24 November, she died.

The police made their way to Thunderbolt's camp but the bushranger was already gone.

This picture of Frederick Ward is published on the Registry of Births, Deaths and Marriages website.

Back to Mary Ann

After Louisa's death, Thunderbolt returned to Mary Ann and it was not long before she was pregnant again. Their third child, Frederick Wordsworth Ward, was born in August 1868. By that time, however, Thunderbolt and Mary Ann had parted for good.

What became of Mary Ann?

After parting from Thunderbolt, Mary Ann returned to her second husband, John Burrows, and with him had four more children. Mary Ann lived in Mudgee until her death in 1905.

9

THE FINAL YEARS

A new apprentice

In January 1868, Thunderbolt took on another young apprentice. William Monckton was the youngest of Thunderbolt's partners; he was only 13 years old when he joined the bushranger. Like Thomas Mason, Will claimed to have been brought up by a stepfather who beat and abused him. He ran away from home and, discovering that the bushranger was in the district, sought to join him. According to Monckton, Thunderbolt tried to dissuade him, insisting that "if I had my time to come over again, I would serve out my sentence on Cockatoo Island, and try afterwards to lead an honest life". Apparently Thunderbolt changed his mind, however, for soon the pair was causing havoc in the New England district together.

Crimes with Monckton

For most of 1868 the partners committed many crimes together. They seemed to have little fear of capture, striking again and again at the same targets.

The first was on 28 January, when Monckton stood aside to watch and learn while Thunderbolt robbed the northern mail near Tamworth. Two days later they held up the same mail coach, with the same driver. The pair spent much of 1868 in the New England district. They robbed Chinese miners on the Bingara goldfields; they bailed up mail coaches, stole horses from stations, held up pubs and travellers and stole cash, clothing and other goods from stores. At Wellingrove they robbed Mr Maund's store – a crime that would lead to Monckton's downfall.

Will Monckton in about 1905, pictured in the book Three Years with Thunderbolt. Accessed through Project Gutenberg.

TWO HUNDRED POUNDS REWARD
FOR THE
APPREHENSION OF FREDERICK WARD,
OTHERWISE KNOWN AS
"THUNDERBOLT,"
AND £50 EACH FOR ACCOMPLICES.

Colonial Secretary's Office,
Sydney, 25th May, 1867.

WHEREAS the abovenamed Convict, who effected his escape from the Penal Establishment, Cockatoo Island, on the 11th September, 1863, is still at large, and is further charged with the commission of divers other serious crimes: And whereas, by notice dated the 4th December, 1865, a Reward of £100 was offered by the Government for the capture of this offender: Notice is hereby given, that an increased Reward of £200 will be paid by the Government for the apprehension of the above named offender, or if effected upon information received, then one-half of the Reward to the person giving such information, and the other moiety to the person or persons effecting the capture; and further, that the Government will pay a Reward of £50, to be similarly divided, for the apprehension of any accomplices of the said Frederick Ward, arrested in his company, or associated with him in the commission of crime.

The above Rewards to be in lieu of all other Rewards payable by the Government under previous notices for the apprehension or conviction of this offender.

4024   HENRY PARKES.

The reward for Thunderbolt's capture increased to £200. From the Maitland Mercury & Hunter River General Advertiser 6 June 1867. NLA Trove 18713990/3.

Three years with Thunderbolt

Forty years after the bushranger's death, Will Monckton wrote an account of their adventures together. In his book, Monckton speaks of Thunderbolt's kindness; of his generosity and his love for his family. Many of the legends that are still believed about Thunderbolt grew from the stories that Monckton told, although many of those stories are not true. Even the title – Three years with Thunderbolt – is a lie, for the pair spent less than a year together.

Rewards for capture

In May 1867 a reward of £200 was offered for the capture of Thunderbolt, and £50 for the capture of any accomplice. By December 1868 this reward had doubled to £400.

Wirth's band: Legend

One of Thunderbolt's most famous crimes was the robbery of Wirth's band. On 19 March 1868 Thunderbolt and Monckton met a band of travelling German musicians on the road to Tamworth. One of the musicians later told the story that Thunderbolt demanded their money but was not happy with the mere £16 that they had. To compensate, Thunderbolt, who was fond of music, ordered them to play. He enjoyed their music for three hours, requesting pieces from the Italian opera. When at last he let them go, the musicians complained that they were poor and could not do without the money he had taken. In response, Thunderbolt wrote down their addresses and promised to return it to them when he came into more money. The story goes that Thunderbolt was true to his word, and when, months later, the band returned to the address they had given him, they found the money waiting for them! Like many of the Thunderbolt stories, however, some of the details have probably been exaggerated.

Myth: Thunderbolt's Leap

Many geographical features in NSW are named after Thunderbolt. Near Emmaville, NSW, is a wide and deep gully known as "Thunderbolt's Leap". It is named after an adventure that Will Monckton narrated – although, like most of his stories, it is a myth.

In Monckton's story, he and Thunderbolt were trying to cross the Tenterfield Creek on horseback when they noticed two policemen in disguise. The bushrangers fled with the police in hot pursuit and firing upon them. They came to a creek with steep banks about 10 metres apart. Thunderbolt charged on, his racehorse leaping across the chasm and landing safely on the other side. Terrified, Monckton tried to follow but his horse fell short into the creek bed. The horse died and Monckton's ankle was broken, but the police gave up the chase and Thunderbolt returned to rescue his young partner.

Robbing the Chinese

Several times Thunderbolt and Monckton robbed the Chinese diggers on the goldfields. Unlike the European diggers, the Chinese rarely carried weapons. Some believe that it was cowardly of Thunderbolt to attack these unarmed men while leaving the armed Europeans alone.

Combo

Thunderbolt only stole the finest racehorses. His favourite was a chestnut thoroughbred with a white blaze named "Combo".

[From *Government Gazette*, 29th December, 1868.]

Colonial Secretary's Office,
Sydney, 24th December, 1868.

£400 REWARD

FOR THE APPREHENSION OF FREDERICK WARD, AND £100 EACH FOR ACCOMPLICES.

WHEREAS the abovenamed convict, who effected his escape from the Penal Establishment, Cockatoo Island, on the 11th September, 1863, is still at large, and is further charged on warrants with the commission of divers other serious crimes; and whereas, by notice dated the 25th May, 1867, a Reward of £200 was offered by Government for the capture of this offender, and a further Reward of £50 for the apprehension of any accomplices of the said Frederick Ward: Notice is hereby given, that an increased Reward of £400 will be paid by the Government for the apprehension of the abovenamed offender, or, if effected upon information received, then one-half of the Reward to the person giving such information, and the other moiety to the person or persons effecting the capture; and further, that the Government will pay a Reward of £100, to be similarly divided, for the apprehension of any accomplices of the said Frederick Ward, arrested in his company, or associated with him in the commission of crime.

The above Rewards to be in lieu of all other Rewards payable by the Government under previous notices for the apprehension or conviction of this offender.

JOHN ROBERTSON.

The reward for Thunderbolt's capture increased to £400. From NSW Police Gazette, 30 Dec 1868, p.376

A drawing of the improbable story of "Thunderbolt's leap", as pictured in the book Three Years with Thunderbolt. Accessed through Project Gutenberg.

Monckton leaves Thunderbolt

By late 1868 William Monckton had had enough of life with Thunderbolt. He left the bushranger and got a job at Wellingrove station, but was soon in trouble again. He was caught trying to steal a mare but was let off with a warning. Only a few days later Monckton was arrested for stealing onions from a farmer's garden. He gave a false name but when the police took him to Maund's store, he was recognised as the boy who had helped Thunderbolt hold up the store some months earlier.

Monckton was charged with attempting to commit robbery under arms. He was found guilty but because of his youth, the court was lenient. He was sentenced to six years' imprisonment. The first year was to be served in Darlinghurst Gaol but for the remaining five he was to attend a Reformatory School.

What became of Monckton?

Monckton was released after one year and went on to live a prosperous life. He settled in Howell, NSW, and became a farmer. Monckton married in 1881 and fathered eleven children.

After Monckton left, Thunderbolt never took on another partner. For over a year he carried on alone, turning up now and then in the New England region to rob a traveller or steal a horse.

Wellingrove, NSW. Thunderbolt and Monckton robbed the store here in 1868; later in the year Monckton left Thunderbolt to work at the Wellingrove station. National Library of Australia an4647816

Death

On 25 May 1870, Thunderbolt was to have his last adventure.

It started near Big Rock (now known as Thunderbolt's Rock): the same place where Ward was shot in the leg soon after his escape from Cockatoo Island.

First Thunderbolt held up Mr and Mrs Blanch, who ran the Royal Oak Hotel near Uralla. They had little money with them so he let them go. Next he robbed a group of travellers and an Italian travelling salesman named Giovanni Cappasotti.

His "business" done, Thunderbolt then ordered his victims into Blanch's Inn and bought drinks for them. While the others stayed to enjoy some drinking, singing and dancing, Cappasotti asked permission to leave. Thunderbolt granted it, warning Cappasotti not to return to Uralla, where there was a police station. The salesman set off in the direction Thunderbolt had ordered him to go, but once out of sight he doubled back to report the robbery to the Uralla police.

Two policemen set out immediately. They were Constable Alexander Binning Walker and Senior Constable John Mulhall. Mulhall's horse was faster than Walker's; he sped ahead and arrived at the inn before his partner. In the meantime, Thunderbolt had taken a liking to a horse that was in the care of a young man named Michael A. Coughlan. He was taking the horse for a trial ride, with an anxious Coughlan riding by his side, when Mulhall appeared. When Thunderbolt saw the policeman he fired a shot and Mulhall fired in return. Mulhall's horse bolted at the sound of gunfire and charged back along the road towards Walker. As he rode past, Mulhall cried out "I have exchanged shots with them. Go on, and shoot the wretch!"

Constable Walker

Walker was off-duty when he went after Thunderbolt. Because he was not in uniform, the bushranger did not know at first that Walker was a policeman.

A drawing of the fatal shoot-out, as pictured in Town and Country Journal, 4 June 1870. State Library of NSW.

Walker took up the challenge. On horseback he chased the bushranger for half an hour or so through the bush. Walker's gun went off accidentally and Thunderbolt returned his fire. At last they came to a waterhole. Thunderbolt dismounted and swam across. Walker shot Thunderbolt's horse dead to remove his means of escape. Walker, still on horseback, then crossed the creek and followed Thunderbolt as he ran further along the bank. Thunderbolt again leaped into the water and had almost arrived at the other side when Walker caught up with him.

The men stood facing each other, with the narrow creek between them. Thunderbolt asked Walker whether he was a trooper and Walker replied that he was. Thunderbolt asked his name and said: "Are you a married man?" When Walker admitted that he was,

Thunderbolt cautioned him to keep back, warning: "remember your family".

Walker asked the bushranger to surrender but Thunderbolt replied "No. I will die first."

Walker then plunged his horse into the creek. As the horse stumbled and went under, Thunderbolt sprang towards Walker. The policeman fired, using his last bullet. It hit Thunderbolt in the chest but he did not die; he struggled with the policeman until Walker hit him on the head with his revolver and the bushranger finally collapsed.

Walker dragged the limp body from the creek and returned to Blanch's Inn. He and Coughlan set out with a cart to fetch Thunderbolt's body but by that time it was dark, and though they searched for three hours they could not find him. The next morning Walker returned with a search party. In the morning light they found Thunderbolt's body and took it to Blanch's Inn for an autopsy, and later to the Uralla Courthouse for public display. A government doctor examined the body and concluded that the dead man was indeed Fred Ward, otherwise known as "Thunderbolt". Several people identified the body, including Will Monckton, who had just been released from gaol and happened to be passing through Armidale soon after Thunderbolt's death. He stated that "I have just seen a dead body lying in the court house: I recognise it as Thunderbolt. I am quite positive it is him, I was with Ward twelve months".

Thunderbolt's death

Thunderbolt died at Kentucky Creek near Uralla.

Thunderbolt's gun

Thunderbolt dropped his gun in the creek during the final struggle. When police later found the gun, they discovered there were no bullets left. They also found that Thunderbolt had tried to shoot it but the gun had misfired.

Thunderbolt's grave in Uralla, picture taken in 2011. Photo courtesy of author.

The autopsy

According to local legend, Thunderbolt's body was disembowelled at his autopsy so that the body would last longer for display to the public. The story goes that his intestines were buried in the back yard of Blanch's Inn, although like so many Thunderbolt myths, we have no proof of this.

The fatal wound

Thunderbolt's autopsy showed that the bullet had entered below his left collarbone near the armpit. It had travelled through both lungs and come out the right side of his chest.

Constable Walker

For his bravery Constable Walker was promoted to Senior Constable. He had a long and successful career; by the time he retired in 1912 he had reached the rank of Superintendent.

Over the next few days hundreds of people came to view the body. People helped themselves to locks of hair for souvenirs. A photographer took pictures of the body and sold them for a shilling each. On 29 May 1870 Thunderbolt was buried on the edge of the Uralla cemetery. His grave was unmarked for decades until 1915, when, responding to popular interest, Uralla citizens raised the money to build a headstone.

Constable Alexander Binning Walker, the policeman who killed Thunderbolt. State Library of NSW 901135.

Controversy

Years after his death people started questioning the true identity of Thunderbolt and asking: who really lies in the grave at Uralla?

Some claim that the man Walker killed was really William Ward – Fred's brother. Some believe that the real Thunderbolt (Fred) attended William's funeral dressed as a woman, with his face concealed behind a veil. He then retrieved his hidden riches from the caves before travelling to the goldfields in San Francisco and later to Canada.

Another story is that Thunderbolt was not Fred Ward but Fred Britten – the other escapee from Cockatoo Island. A strange twist is that late in his life, Will Monckton supported this theory. Although he had identified the dead man's body as Fred Ward, and although he wrote in his book "Three years with Thunderbolt" that Thunderbolt was Fred Ward, he later claimed he had been lying to protect Thunderbolt. He claimed that he had sworn an oath to keep Thunderbolt's real identity a secret for forty years.

Who was Thunderbolt? Whose is the body in the grave at Uralla? There are many myths – stories of letters signed by "Fred" in Thunderbolt's handwriting and sent from Canada long after his supposed death; stories of Thunderbolt being seen at the races days after the killing; stories of an Australian named Fred Ward lying in a Canadian cemetery. All of these are false. The truth is that in 1870 Constable Walker killed Fred Ward, also known as Thunderbolt, and that Ward's body lies dead but not forgotten in the cemetery in Uralla.

A painting of the shooting of Thunderbolt, by Samual Calvert. State Library of Victoria 151384.

A sad ending

Fred Ward was not fond of violence and had no real need to turn to crime. He had great skill with horses as well as intelligence and charm; he could have made an honest living. Instead, unwise choices led him to the life of a bushranger and so he lived his life on the run. His career was long but not very successful; his profits were little more than a few pounds, a saddle, some food or clothing or a horse. He moved from camp to camp, often separated from his family, often cold and uncomfortable and always on the lookout for police. And then, finally as reported in the *Sydney Morning Herald,* he was "shot down like a dog, and so ended a wasted, and worse than wasted, life."

In the years leading up to Thunderbolt's death, the wave of bushranging that had swept the country was gradually drying up due to improved communications, a reformed police force, and a hardening of community attitudes towards lawlessness. With Thunderbolt's death, New South Wales' age of bushranging was finally at an end.

Frederick Ward, or "Captain Thunderbolt", photographed after his death in 1870 by A. Cunningham. National Library of Australia Trove 168716102.

THUNDERBOLT
by Pannifex & Cumming

There's a graveyard in Uralla,
That's in New South Wales you know,
Where a highwayman was buried
Many, many years ago.
Thunderbolt his tombstone names him,

He who rides the road at night,
Those who've met him in the moonlight
Say he's Thunderbolt all right!

Refrain.

Thunderbolt! It's Thunderbolt!
Riding to Uralla,
From the Moonbi Ranges
As he used to ride of yore;
The past returns to meet him,
And his ghostly friends to greet him,
But he needn't fear the troopers.
He is safe for ever more!

People loved this handsome outlaw,
People loved him far and wide,
Tried to guard him from the troopers
When he roamed the countryside.
Housewives used to hang a blanket
As a signal on the line.–

Red ones said "Look Out for troopers!"
White ones asked him in to dine!

Came the day that shocked New England,
Someone told the police he'd seen
Thunderbolt with pals at Blanche's
Raising glasses to the Queen.
Swift the troopers rode to take him,
Even to this day folk speak

Of the way the trooper shot him,
Shot him by Kentucky Creek.

There's a legend in New England,
Thunderbolt has never died,
Still he haunts the Moonbi Ranges
And the lovely countryside.
Folk declare that they have seen him
When the moon is on the wane,
Riding like a flash of lightning
To Uralla once again!

Thunderbolt's death certificate.

SOURCES: THUNDERBOLT

Books and websites:

Baxter, C. (2011). *Captain Thunderbolt & his lady: the true story of bushrangers Frederick Ward & Mary Ann Bugg.* Sydney: Allen & Unwin.

Baxter, C. (2012) *Bushranger Frederick Ward (Captain) Thunderbolt and Mary Ann Bugg.* http://thunderboltb ushranger.com.au/index.html [Accessed 15/10/13]

Brouwer, D. (2002). *Thunderbolt: horse-breaker to bushranger.* Tocal: CB Alexander Foundation.

Cummins, B. (1988). *Thunderbolt: a biography of the last of New South Wales' notorious bushrangers.* Moree: R.K. Cummins.

Hobden, J. (1988). *Thunderbolt.* Tamworth: Jim Hobden.

Williams, S. (1987). *A ghost called Thunderbolt: the career and legend of Frederick Ward, bushranger throughout northern New South Wales.* Woden, ACT: Popinjay.

Newspapers:

Maitland Mercury & Hunter River General Advertiser
15 July 1854
22 Dec 1863

18 April 1865
25 April 1865
2 May 1865
16 Dec 1865
9 Jan 1866
29 March 1866
16 June 1866
28 Aug 1866
12 Jan 1867
12 Feb 1867
16 Feb 1867
5 March 1867
21 May 1867
28 May 1867
1 October 1867
21 Jan 1868
26 Jan 1869
7 June 1870
19 July 1870
30 March 1882

Sydney Morning Herald
28 Dec 1865
6 April 1866
7 April 1866
11 May 1866
14 April 1869
4 June 1870

The Queenslander
25 May 1867

The Mercury
1 June 1867

Armidale Express
28 May 1870

Registry of Births, Deaths and Marriages NSW

Death certificate of Frederick Wordsworth Ward

NSW Police Gazette and Weekly Record of Crime

14 Oct, 21 Oct, 4 Nov, 11 Nov 1863
30 Dec 1868
1 March 1871
3 June 1874

BACK COVER MATERIAL

Captain Thunderbolt

Frederick Wordsworth Ward, better known as 'Captain Thunderbolt', was bushranger who plaughed New South Wales for almost seven years during one of the longest bushranging 'careers' in history. Thunderbolt was intelligent, charming and courageous; a great storyteller who enjoyed much public support.

Although a horse thief and a highway robber, he has become something of a romantic figure of Australia's past. Many legends have grown up around him – stories of a devoted husband and father, a gentleman, a lover of music and literature; a man who hated violence and a victim of the law. The truth, however, is quite a different story.

This book provide a brief biography of Thunderbolt's life and some of his more notable exploits, and refutes many of the popular myths that surround him.

A

accomplices, *34, 36, 38, 39, 47, 49, 65, 67, 68*

apprentices,
  see Mason, Thomas;
  Monckton, William,

B

Bell, James, *49, 54*
Big Rock, *17, 20*
Bonshaw Hotel, *70, 71*
Britten, Fred, *15, 17*
Bugg, Mary Ann see Mary Ann Bull, the, *34, 45*
bushranger, gentleman, *39*
bushranging career, slow start, *29, 32*
bushranging epidemic, *20*

C

captive woman, *38, 56*
capture, almost, *36*
cheques, *39, 42*
Cockatoo Island prison, *15*
  escape, *15, 17*
  myth about escape, *15*
crime, driven to, *51*

crime wave of December 1865, *49, 51*
crimes continue, *47, 58*
crimes with Monckton,

D

death,
driven to crime, *51*

E

escape from prison, *2, 15*

F

fatal wound,

G

gang, first, *34, 36, 38, 39, 42*
gang, second, *47, 49, 51, 54*
gentleman bushranger, *39*
grave,
gun,
  myth, *36*

H

Healey, Thomas, *34*
Hogan, Thomas, *34, 45*
hold-up, first, *24, 26, 28, 29*
horseman, expert, *73*

Printed in Great Britain
by Amazon